LOOK OUT FOR TURTLES!

Galapagos Turtles

by MELVIN BERGER
illustrated by MEGAN LLOYD

HarperCollins Publishers

The *Let's-Read-and-Find-Out Science* book series was originated by Dr. Franklyn M. Branley, Astronomer Emeritus and former Chairman of the American Museum–Hayden Planetarium, and was formerly co-edited by him and Dr. Roma Gans, Professor Emeritus of Childhood Education, Teachers College, Columbia University. Text and illustrations for each of the books in the series are checked for accuracy by an expert in the relevant field. For a complete catalog of Let's-Read-and-Find-Out Science books, write to HarperCollins Children's Books, 10 East 53rd Street, New York, NY 10022.

LOOK OUT FOR TURTLES!

Library of Congress Cataloging-in-Publication Data
Berger, Melvin.
    Look out for turtles / by Melvin Berger ; illustrated by Megan Lloyd.
        p.   cm. — (Let's-read-and-find-out science book)
    Summary: Describes the remarkable turtle that can live almost anywhere, eat almost anything, range in size from tiny to gigantic, and live longer than any other animal.
        ISBN 0-06-022539-4. — ISBN 0-06-022540-8 (lib. bdg.)
        ISBN 0-06-445156-9 (pbk.)
    1. Turtles—Juvenile literature.   [1. Turtles.]   I. Lloyd, Megan, ill.
II. Title.   III. Series.
QL666.C5B44   1992   90-36894
597.92—dc20   CIP
                                                                    AC

The art in this book was done with pen and ink and watercolor on D'Arches cold-press watercolor paper.

Red-Footed Tortoise

Most land turtles move very, v·e·r·y slowly.

Suppose you ran a one-mile race with a turtle. You would cross the finish line in about ten or fifteen minutes. The turtle would get there about five hours later!

3

But did you know that some turtles can move very fast? These turtles live in the ocean. They have flippers instead of legs. Some sea turtles can swim a mile in less than three minutes. The very fastest human swimmer takes five minutes to swim a mile.

Loggerhead Turtle

Turtles—on land and in the sea—are among the oldest living creatures in the world. They have been on earth for nearly 200 million years! Turtles were here at the time of the mighty dinosaurs. And they are still here today.

Why have turtles survived so long?

Many turtles have hard shells. The shell is the turtle's house. It is also its shield. The hard shell protects the turtle from its enemies.

When danger is near, most land turtles hide inside their shells. They pull in their heads, tails, and all four legs. Now the turtle is safe from harm.

Wood Turtle

The turtle's shell has two main parts. The top part is called the *carapace*. The bottom is the *plastron*. The carapace and plastron are joined by a *bridge*. The bridge has openings for the head, tail, and legs.

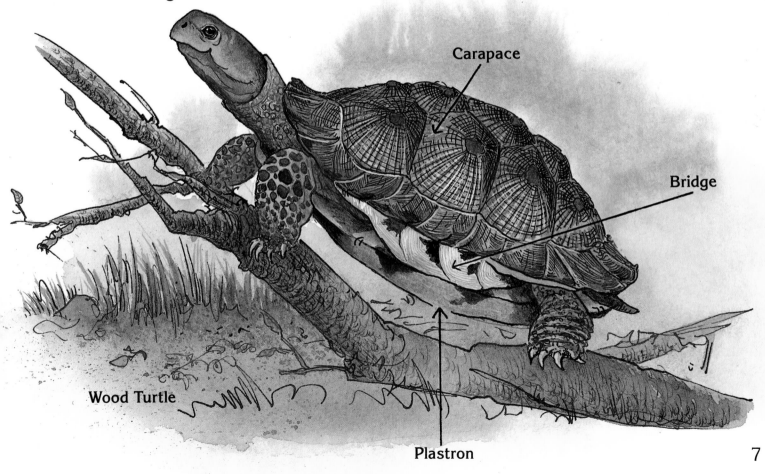

Carapace

Bridge

Wood Turtle

Plastron

The box turtle and mud turtle have a special kind of shell. When the turtle is inside, it pulls the carapace and plastron together! The two parts close up tightly. You can't slip even a penny inside.

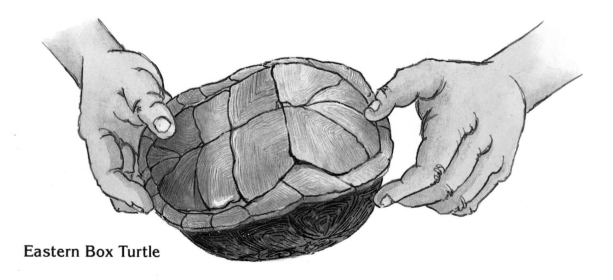

Eastern Box Turtle

8

Eastern Box Turtle

The carapace helps turtles to hide in another way. Many kinds of
land turtles have a mixture of colors on their carapaces. Brown,
yellow, green, gray, or black are common. The different colors blend
in with the turtle's surroundings.

A water turtle's carapace is usually dark in color. Water turtles swim so fast that they don't need colorful carapaces to hide them from their enemies.

Common Snapping Turtle

On soil, sand, or mud—
on grass, rocks, or logs—
in ponds, streams, or the sea—

Leaf Turtle

—turtles can be very hard to spot.

Common Snapping Turtle

Turtles don't have teeth. But they can bite with their strong jaws.
A turtle bite can hurt an animal or a human being.

Turtles have survived for millions of years for other reasons. They can live almost anywhere, and eat many different foods. Those that live in or near ponds and streams eat water plants, bugs, snails, and fish.

Desert Tortoise

Turtles that live on land—or tortoises, as they are sometimes
called—eat plants, fruit, insects, vegetables, and worms.

14

Green Turtle

Turtles that live in the sea eat seaweed, jellyfish, crabs, and fish.

Most turtles that live in cold climates sleep during the winter months. They hibernate. Some dig themselves into the mud on the bottom of a lake or river. Others snuggle into the soil on land. There they stay until spring.

Sea turtles in cold climates swim to warmer waters when the temperature drops too low.

Eastern Box Turtle

In March and April, the land turtles begin to come out of their
winter homes. Over the next few months the male and female
turtles mate. The female then digs a hole in the ground for a nest.
Even turtles that live in the sea crawl up on land to make their nests.

17

Green Turtle

The female lays a "clutch" of eggs in the nest. The number of eggs in each clutch varies. The African pancake turtle lays just one egg at a time. The green turtle lays up to 150 eggs in her clutch.

After she lays the eggs, the female turtle covers them with soil or sand. And she leaves.

18

For two or three months the turtles grow inside the eggs. By the end of the summer the eggs are ready to hatch.

The baby turtle uses its sharp egg tooth to slit open the eggshell. It takes from one to four days to open the egg and pull itself out. The baby turtle loses its egg tooth after a few weeks.

Green Turtles

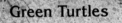

Green Turtles

The newborn turtles have little protection. Their shells are very soft, so they must get to a safe hiding place quickly. They go as fast as their stubby legs or flippers can carry them.

Tiny sea turtles head right for the ocean. Somehow they know the way. Usually they make the trip at night. Even so, many are caught and eaten by crabs and gulls.

Young land turtles have to watch out, too. Raccoons, birds, dogs, and foxes can easily catch and eat them.

Eastern Box Turtles

Marion's Tortoise

Turtles live longer than most other animals. One turtle lived to be about 170 years old. A soldier found this turtle on an island in the Indian Ocean in 1766. It was already fully grown when he took it to his camp. The turtle lived there for 152 years. In 1918 it was killed accidentally. No one knows how much longer it might have lived.

Turtles range in size from tiny to gigantic. Among the smallest are the mud turtles. They grow to be between three and six inches long.

Eastern Mud Turtle
(actual size)

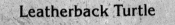
Leatherback Turtle

The biggest are the seagoing leatherback turtles. One amazing leatherback turtle was found off the coast of California in 1961. It was nearly 6 feet long! And it weighed close to 1,300 pounds.

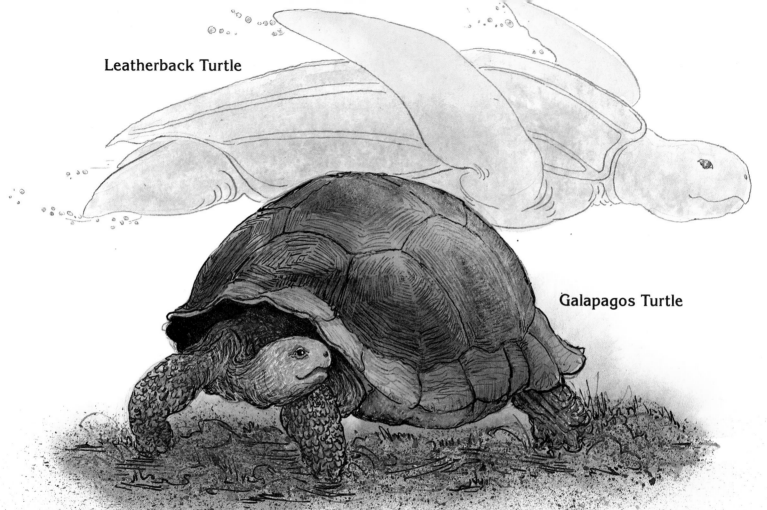

Leatherback Turtle

Galapagos Turtle

The Galapagos turtle takes the prize for largest land turtle. At 4 feet long it is about two thirds the length of the leatherback. This turtle weighs an average of 600 pounds.

Turtles are survivors.

—Most have hard shells to protect them.

—Their carapaces help keep them out of sight.

—Different kinds of turtles can exist almost anywhere on land or in the sea.

—Various sorts of turtles can eat many different kinds of plants and animals.

—And some live to be more than 100 years old.

Diamondback Terrapin

27

Yet every year fewer and fewer turtles are left on earth. Many are killed by humans. Some people eat the flesh and eggs of turtles. And people make combs and ornaments from their shells.

People also build houses, roads, and factories on land where turtles live. Without room to wander, find food, and lay eggs, the turtles die.

Turtles are killed by pollution, too. As we dump poisons on the land and in the water, we kill turtles.

Eastern Painted Turtle

29

Bog Turtle

Some types of turtles have already died out. The Kemp's ridley is nearly extinct, and other sea turtles are endangered. Some land turtles, like the bog turtle, are endangered, too. Once gone, these turtles will never come back.

You and I have an important job to do. We must

—not harm any turtles we find;

—save turtles we find on roadways by carrying them to safety;

—help to protect and clean up the land and water where turtles live;

—ask for laws to prevent sea turtles from being caught in large fishing nets.

Spotted Turtle

31

Eastern Painted Turtle

By doing our job well, we can help turtles survive for another 200 million years!